Maritime Great Yar

Volume I

C000107971

A Portrait in Old Photographs and Postcards

by

Peter Allard and Parry Watson

S. B. Publications

*This book is dedicated to all the photographers, many unknown,
without whose efforts this book would have been impossible to produce.*

First published in 1995 by S.B. Publications
c/o 19 Grove Road, Seaford, East Sussex, BN25 1TP.

© Copyright 1995 Peter Allard and Parry Watson.

All rights reseved.

ISBN 1 85770 082 1

Typeset and printed by Geo. R. Reeve Ltd.
9-11 Town Green, Wymondham, Norfolk, NR18 0BD. (01953) 602297.

CONTENTS

Front Cover: A busy scene on the River Yare in October 1905. The paddle tug *Gleaner* is towing out five Scottish drifters including one from Kirkcaldy, a white-funnelled steam drifter the *Marie* YH 717 has just turned the bend heading for the fishwharf with paddle tug *Express* just astern. On the extreme right the bows of the North Shields, steam drifter *Kitty* SN 308 can be seen. In the background a large Dutch timber vessel from Terneuzen the *Henry* is prominent with attendant Thames sailing barges alongside.

ACKNOWLEDGEMENTS

I would like to acknowledge the great help over many years of Parry Watson, a person who knows perhaps more than anybody about the history of shipping and particularly the herring industry at Great Yarmouth. This book would have been incomplete without his help and advice, and for this reason his name appears on the front cover. I would also like to thank the following for all their help in various ways: Steven Allard, Barry Banham, Diane Kapoor and Andy Wallis. Also to Steve Benz for additional editing and marketing and many others not mentioned by name.

THE AUTHORS

PETER ALLARD has long been interested in maritime Great Yarmouth. His great-grandfather owned two local steam drifters and his grandfather worked on the fishwharf in its heyday. He has collected information on the fishing industry, particularly the sailing drifters and trawlers for many years and has an extensive collection of photographs. This is his second book.

PARRY WATSON is an acknowledged authority on Yarmouth's maritime history and is employed by the Great Yarmouth Port Authority. Interested in ships from an early age, his extensive collection of old photographs of the fishing industry is unique.

INTRODUCTION

The port of Great Yarmouth has seen many changes over the years. Situated on the east coast midway between the Thames and Humber estuaries, Great Yarmouth was built upon its herring fisheries and owes its very existence to that luscious delicacy. While the herring fishery was the stable industry at Yarmouth, trawling for white fish was being introduced in the 1840s.

Within 40 years, Yarmouth was the most important trawling port in England, with huge investments being made. For a number of years, the total number of Yarmouth-based sailing smacks outnumbered those at Hull and even Grimsby. Although most of the fish caught was shipped direct to Billingsgate, Shadwell and Columbia fish markets in London, the fleets were based at Yarmouth. These fleets were vast and owned by large companies, including the North Sea Trawling Company Limited, Morgan Brothers, Samuel Smith, The Great Yarmouth Steam Carrying Company and F.S. and J. Leleu. The famous Short Blue Fleet owned by Hewett and Company of Barking, Essex, was based at Gorleston and at its peak had a fleet of over 240 sailing smacks, steam trawlers and steam carriers. All these huge fleets had disappeared by the turn of the century. Remarkably, all went bankrupt within a period of 15 years.

The herring fishing was booming, however, and steam was being introduced into the industry. Local yards turned to building steam drifters and others came from the Tyne and the west coast. At its peak, up to the outbreak of the First World War in 1914, Yarmouth was the largest herring port in the world. Over one thousand drifters fished from the port, many coming down from Scottish ports such as Peterhead, Aberdeen and Fraserburgh.

With all these fishing fleets, especially the earlier sailing vessels, there was a constant need for paddle tugs. Several firms were established and there was much rivalry. Later, screw tugs were introduced, but the fleets were much depleted by then. The port of Yarmouth had several well established shipyards and drydocks and all were integrated into the fishing industry for many years.

Trinity House had an important base in Yarmouth which serviced the numerous lightships. Trinity House tenders were also based here. The harbour was well known for its timber imports as well as general cargo. All manner of vessels landed their cargoes at the quaysides.

Since Yarmouth was a well-known holiday town, the harbour saw a variety of passenger pleasure vessels, both for seaborne excursions and inland for the Norfolk Broads. There were regular in-season daily trips to London for many years. These trips were often well patronised.

Numerous shallow sand banks lay off the East Anglian coast, many especially close to Great Yarmouth. Shipping disasters were all too common and lifeboat stations were established at Caister, Yarmouth Seafront and Gorleston. These complimented the harbour tugs for lifesaving and salvage work.

This book has tried to bring together much of the business of the port of Great Yarmouth as it was around the turn of the century. A few photographs and postcards are perhaps earlier or later, but it was then that it was at its peak of activity. Never again will we see fleets of sailing smacks leaving harbour hundreds at a time or be able to virtually walk across a river tightly packed with steam drifters. These were perhaps the halcyon days of Great Yarmouth.

Peter R. Allard
Great Yarmouth

A TOPSAIL SCHOONER AT BOLLARD QUAY, 1880s

A topsail schooner lays off at Bollard, Southtown, in the 1880s. These vessels were once a common sight in harbour, bringing coal from north-eastern ports. Bessey and Palmer of Yarmouth had a large fleet of sailing colliers just before the turn of the century. One of the last sailing colliers was the *Madeleine*, 91 tons, built in 1845 at Yarmouth. She was towed down river in September 1904 to be broken up. Two small fishing smacks, one cutter rigged, lay opposite on the Yarmouth side.

SAILING VESSELS, SOUTH AND WEST QUAYS, 1890s

Sailing vessels lay at their moorings in the upper part of the harbour at South Quay and at West Quay in the 1890s. Note the floating logs of timber on the right. Steam began to make an impact at Yarmouth in the 1840s with the first steam tugs. Steam trawlers entered the scene in the 1880s and the first steam drifter appeared in the late 1890s. All the local sailing fishing fleet had departed by the outbreak of the First World War.

GORLESTON QUAYSIDE, 1890s

Gorleston Quayside in the early 1890s with sailing vessels. This is believed to be taken close to the foot of Ice House Hill, or further south towards Baker Street, as a slipway is in evidence. The dismasted smack YH 308 is *Jessica,* 43 tons, built in 1868 and owned in turn by W.H. Makepeace of Yamouth, W. Soards and Hewett & Co Ltd, both of Gorleston. She does not appear in the 1894 register and is presumed to have been broken up by then.

ON THE LOOK-OUT AT GORLESTON, 1890s

Two veteran mariners, presumably from the Gorleston beach companies, check shipping movements with an old brass telescope from the end of Gorleston South Pier in the 1890s. Both are leaning on the old wooden hand-capstan used for assisting in sailing vessels at the harbour entrance. In the background is the old Gorleston Pier Lighthouse demolished in the early 1960s.

SAILING SHIPS AND PADDLE TUGS, 1890s

This photograph dates from the early 1890s and is taken from the Southtown side of the river near what is now Richard's Dry Dock and looking north towards South Quay. The upper ferryman is rowing back across to South Quay, which is lined with sailing vessels and paddle tugs. The right-hand vessel is *Flying Childers,* built in 1864 at South Shields. On the Southtown side, a young lad is watching timber vessels unload at Jewson's Quay from the stern of a fishing smack.

GORLESTON BOATMEN, 1890s

Gorleston boatmen discuss maritime matters near their yawls and other boats about 1895. The Ranger Company look-out and watch-house stands beside the lighthouse, which was erected in 1886. Gorleston had three beach companies at this time, the Storm Company, the Ranger Company and the Young Flies, all of which had their own yawls, lifeboats and look-outs. The black cloud has been superimposed.

THE OLD HAVEN BRIDGE, c.1910

The old Haven Bridge with a clinker-built Norfolk wherry about to pass underneath about 1910. This bridge was built in 1854 and opened amidst great ceremony on October 21st. It cost nearly £60,000 to build and had an opening span of 50 feet and two side spans of 65 feet each. The bridge finally closed on February 20th, 1928, a temporary wooden bridge standing alongside until the present bridge opened in October 1930.

GORLESTON QUAYSIDE, c.1901

Looking north at Gorleston Quayside from the top of the lighthouse about 1901. Note the absence of the King William the Fourth public house from its present position. The old King William the Fourth building was situated, as can be seen, further away from the quayside to the west. A building presumably connected with the fishing industry occupies its present position. Many people are out for a weekend stroll, and a Gorleston-to-Yarmouth steamer is preparing to take on passengers.

GORLESTON QUAYSIDE, 1905

Brush Quay, Gorleston, looking north in 1905. Note the tramlines of the Gorleston beach to Southtown tramway, which have just been laid. Rowing-boats line the quayside whilst two beach company look-outs can be detected. The nearest on the left is that of the Storm Company, which surprisingly survived until 1983, and alongside the lighthouse can just be seen the Ranger Company look-out.

FLOODS AT GORLESTON, 1905

A similar view of Brush Quay, Gorleston, on January 8th, 1905 after a tidal surge following strong northerly winds the previous day. Most of Gorleston Quayside is under a considerable depth of water. The paddle tug in midstream with a work boat astern is *King Edward VII,* owned by Nicholson Towage Ltd. Note the men paddling and walking in knee-deep water close to Quayside.

STEAM COASTER BEING LAUNCHED, 1923

The steam coaster *Coniscrag* being launched from Pitcher's yard at North Quay in February 1923, the second and last vessel to be built at this site. The first was the *Braemore* in July 1921. In 1924 this firm went into voluntary liquidation and the frames of the two steel vessels on the stocks were purchased for 96 guineas for breaking up. This yard was known as the Bowling Green Shipyard. On the right in the background are boatsheds at Cobholm.

SAILING BOATS, YARMOUTH BEACH, c.1900

Sea trips were very popular from Yarmouth Central Beach in late Victorian and Edwardian times. These beach boats resembled the older beach yawls, although for ease of handling they were often cutter rigged. This particular boat no. 20 belonged to James Amiss, who owned four beach vessels, *The Duchess of Edinburgh, Grace Darling,* the *Star of the East* and *Moss Rose.* The last sailing beach vessel, the *Cambria,* 37 feet long and oak, built by William Spence of Southtown in 1891, was sold on September 22nd 1926 for £62-10s (£62.50).

YACHTING STATION,
GT YARMOUTH.

YARMOUTH YACHT STATION, c.1910

A forest of masts at Yarmouth Yacht Station about 1910, with pleasure wherries, sailing yachts and one small pleasure steamer on the extreme right. Many of these vessels stayed overnight here and continued their journey through the Norfolk rivers and broads the next day. Pleasure wherries could be hired here for many years until at least 1915.

SOUTH QUAY, 1920s

South Quay in the 1920s, with town hall and steam coaster *Bullfinch* of London. Owned by the General Steam Navigation Company Ltd. of London, *Bullfinch* was a regular visitor to Yarmouth and Norwich with cargoes of coal and general cargo. Virtually all vessels of this company had black funnels. Note the kiosk and flag of one of the pleasure steamer companies on the quayside.

SAILING SHRIMPERS, c.1912

Sailing shrimpers in the river Bure between the railway bridge and the old suspension bridge about 1912. Sailing shrimpers were once a familiar sight at Yarmouth, their season beginning early in the spring and continuing until mid-October. Extreme left is YH 329 and centre is YH 671 *Coronation*, built in 1902 and owned by the Liffen family for a great many years. Motorised in 1920, one of her last tasks was to take barrels of beer to the remote Berney Arms Pub at the head of Breydon Water in the 1960's.

CREW OF SAILING DRIFTER, c.1900

The crew of the Yarmouth sailing drifter *Girl's Own* YH 462, built at Lowestoft in 1892, at Yarmouth fish wharf just after the turn of the century. This lugger, as sailing drifters were known, was eventually sold to Norway in May 1913. She was unfortunately lost in passage with three hands on board following storms in the North Sea. Her last local owner was James Tidman of Gorleston who had connections with the famous Short Blue Fleet.

A SAILING WOLDER, c.1895

A sailing wolder *Guide Me* YH 532, owned by the Moore family of Yarmouth, moves down river. This photograph, a rare view, is believed to have been taken before the turn of the century. Note the raking stern of the wolder. In the background is Darby's Hard, Gorleston, where many smacks were hauled up and overhauled. This hard was also used for ship breaking and many old smacks and steam drifters ended their days here.

CREW OF SAILING DRIFTER, c.1905

The crew of the Yarmouth sailing drifter *Our Boys* YH 347, line up for the cameraman at the fishwharf about 1905. Built by the firm of Howes and Chapman of South Quay, she was launched in July 1903, the last sailing drifter built in Yarmouth. Built for J.T. Moore of Yarmouth, she was eventually lost on Gorleston beach during the early hours of May 6th, 1913 following a fishing trip.

COMPLETION OF SAILING DRIFTER, 1893

The crew and family of the sailing drifter *Speranza* YH 382, 40 tons gross, in 1893, after her completion at Beeching's Yard at Yarmouth. Built by H. Reynolds at Lowestoft for Robert Plummer of Caister, she saw good service for her owners until replaced by a steam drifter of the same name in 1911. Beeching Brothers built more sailing drifters at Yarmouth than any other firm, their last being *Girl Jane* YH 677 in May 1902 for A. R. Daniels of Yarmouth.

FISHING SMACKS AND LUGGERS, 1890s

Fishing smacks and luggers moored on both sides of the River Yare prior to the turn of the century. The nearest vessels are moored at Bollard Quay and YH 19 is *Spero Expecto* built in 1865. She was lengthened in 1885 and for many years owned by Hewett & Co of Gorleston and Barking, owners of the Short Blue Fleet. Hewett & Co closed its Gorleston premises in 1903, but continued with several steam trawlers under the new name of Brand & Co.

SAILING TRAWLER ENTERING HARBOUR, 1890s

A Yarmouth sailing trawler of the Short Blue Fleet, the *Prosperous* YH 665 entering harbour in the 1890s. *Prosperous* was built in 1876, weighed 70 tons and was owned by Hewett & Co Ltd. of Gorleston and Barking. These vessels were out in fleets for an eight-week period, fishing the Dogger Bank and Clay Deeps grounds and delivering their fish to steam carriers to take to Billingsgate Market.

THE HARBOUR, GORLESTON.

LEAVING HARBOUR AT GORLESTON, c.1890

A common sight prior to 1900, a sailing trawler of the Gorleston-based Short Blue Fleet being towed out to sea whilst onlookers gather at the end of Gorleston Pier. The trawling smack is *Ruby* YH 657, built in Southtown by Fleming Hewett and lengthened in 1887. The *Ruby* was lost in the North Sea fishing grounds on November 16th, 1891 following a collision. The steam screw tug towing out *Ruby* may be *Princess May*.

On the Jetty, Gorleston-on-Sea.

TRAWLING SMACKS HEAD FOR THE SEA, c.1895

Local trawling smacks being towed out to sea before the turn of the century. Steam tugs where allowed to tow a maximum of six smacks, but it was all too common for other smacks to hitch a lift at the rear of the procession. Gorleston South Pier was a popular spot to view the comings and goings of the fishing fleet, especially on a warm day at the weekend. The gentleman on the right appears to be in his "Sunday Best".

SAILING DRIFTER IN FULL SAIL, c.1900

The Yarmouth sailing drifter *Primula* YH 378 in full sail. She was built at Beeching Brothers Yard at Yarmouth in 1893 and was 40 tons gross. Owned by Charles F. Johnson of Yarmouth for many years, *Primula* was eventually sold to Norway in February 1911 along with three other sailing drifters. Sailing drifters continued at Yarmouth until 1915 when *Percy* YH 727, built 1902, finally left for Scandinavian owners.

MISSION VESSEL AT SOUTHTOWN, c.1890

The Royal National Mission to Deep Sea Fishermen smack *Clulow,* formaly LO 357, leaves her Southtown base about 1890. *Clulow* was built in 1884 and is seen here fitted out as a hospital ship for the fishing fleets, hence the absence of fishing numbers on her sides. The Mission moved its headquarters from Southtown to Gorleston in 1899, and three years later *Clulow* was up for sale along with two other Mission Smacks. Bought by Dutch interests, she was known to be still afloat in 1956.

MISSION VESSEL LEAVING HARBOUR, 1930s

The *Sir William Archibald* LO 401 Mission vessel leaving harbour, probably in the 1930s. Owned by the Royal National Mission to Deep Sea Fishermen and Gorleston based, she was built at Fellow's Yard, Southtown in 1927. The *Sir William Archibald* was the last East Anglian sailing trawler built. After wartime service at Scapa Flow, she was back at Gorleston in September 1945, but was eventually sold to Norwegian interests in May 1947.

W. Mason   First Aid Mission Ship, "Sir Edward P. Wills."   Yarmouth

MISSION VESSEL OFF YARMOUTH, 1938

The Mission Vessel *Sir Edward P. Wills* steams off Yarmouth in 1938. Built in Goole in 1937 and owned by the Royal National Mission to Deep Fishermen, she remained in service until 1947. During the second world war, *Sir Edward P. Wills* was used as an examination vessel at Yarmouth, still retaining her old crew. The former Mission buildings at Gorleston, opened in 1899, remain today and are situated at the top of Ice House Hill.

SCOTTISH SAILING DRIFTERS HEAD FOR THE SEA, c.1910

Action in the River Yare about 1910. Kirkcaldy sailing drifters being rowed out of harbour by the crew whilst the Yarmouth-built paddle tug *Yare* tows out another Scottish sailing drifter. Yet another tug, a smaller vessel is astern of the *Yare* towing out several more sailing drifters. The Scottish sailing drifters which arrived in Yarmouth each autumn were known either as Fifies or Zulus, the latter having a long raking stern.

SCOTTISH SAILING DRIFTER c.1906

Scottish sailing and steam drifters arrived in Yarmouth each autumn to fish for herring. This vessel is Banff registered. Others came from Peterhead, Fraserburgh, Buckie, Kirkcaldy and Inverness. The photograph date is probably about 1906 as by 1912, the majority of Scottish drifter owners had invested in steam propulsion. Some sailing drifters were also converted into motor-driven vessels, the first appearing in 1905.

YARMOUTH FISHWHARF, c.1904

Yarmouth fishwharf with buyers waiting for more herring boats to arrive, about 1904. The fishwharf and market were constructed in 1867. Prior to this, herring and trawl fish were landed on the beach close to the jetty. A gentleman with bowler hat sits on a herring swill basket so characteristic of the town. These herring baskets were used only at Yarmouth and nowhere else. Several steam drifters can be seen in the background.

The Fish Market, Great Yarmouth.

HUNDREDS OF HERRING SWILLS, c.1908

The fish market at Yarmouth from a postcard dated 1908. This is a typical scene on a busy day with hundreds of herring swills on the quayside, full of fish. A forest of masts line the quay while one or two funnels of steam drifters can be detected. Herring swills were made at Yarmouth by several firms, the last being Stanley Bird of Southgates Road.

FELLOW'S QUAYSIDE, 1920s

Fellows & Co. quayside at Southtown in the 1920s with a vintage van and steam drifter *Helpmate* YH 129, built at Lowestoft in 1912 and owned for many years by Great Yarmouth Fisheries Ltd. The *Helpmate* was an early casualty in the Second World War and was lost as a result of enemy action on 1 April, 1940. A considerable number of both Yarmouth and Lowestoft drifters and trawlers were lost in action in both world wars, many through striking mines.

STEAM DRIFTERS BECOME TRAWLERS, 1923

Steam drifters turn trawlers. A view of Yarmouth trawl market with trawlers alongside in 1923. The trawl market was situated north of the Fish Wharf and on view is *Ralph Hall Caine* YH 447 and *Eastholme* YH 22 with others astern. Trawling ventures were never successful at Yarmouth despite many attempts. The small crane on the left, built in 1903, was used to unload coal to Yarmouth Gasworks.

SCOTTISH DRIFTERS AT SOUTH QUAY, OCTOBER 1931

Scottish fishermen never fished on Sundays at Yarmouth. Many of their vessels resorted to Yarmouth South Quay to lay up for the weekend. This view in October 1931, looking north towards the town hall, shows steam drifters six abreast for a considerable distance. Extreme left is a steam drifter from Buckie and extreme right is one from Inverness. The four between are from Peterhead. Two Thames sailing barges lay on the Southtown side.

STEAM DRIFTERS ON THE MOVE, EARLY 1930s

Steam drifters on the move. This photograph dates from the early 1930s as the tug *Tactful* can be seen in the background alongside the quay at Gorleston. Two Peterhead steam drifters, one arriving and the other departing, are at the bend in the river. On the left is *June Rose* PD 592, built 1918, and on the right is *Ugievale* PD 202, built 1919. The last Scottish steam drifter to work out of Yarmouth was the *Ocean Raleigh* PD 139 in the home fishing of 1957.

A BUSY DAY AT THE FISHWHARF, c.1935

A very busy October day at Yarmouth fishwharf about 1935. Buyers are looking for fresh herring just landed from the Lowestoft steam drifter *Lord Rodney* LT 390, whilst alongside the Scottish Peterhead steam drifter *Rosebay* PD 65 begins to take on bunkers. The *Rosebay* came into Yarmouth registration in March 1951 as YH 78, her owner being John Plummer of Caister. Sold to Gordon Haylett in 1956, *Rosebay* was broken up in 1961 in Holland.

ARRIVAL OF A YARMOUTH STEAM DRIFTER, 1930s

A scene of grandeur. A Yarmouth steam drifter, the *Harry Eastick,* arrives at the harbour entrance from the fishing grounds with herring in a moderate swell followed by hundreds of hungry gulls. The *Harry Eastick* was the last wooden Yarmouth steam drifter built, being launched from the Yare Dry Dock Company Yard in March 1926. Owned by the Eastick family at Gorleston, she was sold to Dutch shipbreakers in April 1961.

GUTTING HERRING. GT. YARMOUTH.

SCOTTISH GIRLS GUTTING HERRING, 1930s

Scottish girls gutting herring in the 1930s at South Denes. These Scots girls worked on both sides of the River Yare at the height of the great autumn herring fishery. Working in teams of three, two gutting and one packing, and with razor knives flashing at lightning speed, the three could deal with as many as 50 herrings a minute.

SCOTTISH GIRLS AMONGST THE BARRELS, c.1912

Scottish girls take a break and pose for the cameraman among the barrels at Yarmouth South Denes prior to the First World War. They were always called girls irrespective of age. Many came from the ports of Peterhead, Fraserburgh, Kirkcaldy, Banff and Buckie, arriving in hundreds in late September and departing for home in December. Many took presents with them from Yarmouth.

SMALLEST PADDLE TUG IN YARMOUTH, c.1894

The smallest paddle tug owned at Yarmouth, the *Wards,* towing out five sailing smacks about 1894. The *Wards* was owned by E.A. Durrant of South Quay. Built in 1857, it was at Newcastle and Grimsby before coming to Yarmouth. Sold for only £25 in 1896, *Wards* was broken up at Yarmouth the same year. The smack on the left is YH 825 *Phoenix,* also owned by E.A. Durrant.

THE PADDLE TUG *CUPID*, c.1894

A little larger than *Wards* was the paddle tug *Cupid,* another of E.A. Durrant's tugs. She is seen here with three smacks at the harbour bend on her way to sea. Built in 1865 at North Shields, she was at Grangemouth for many years before coming to Yarmouth. For a short period, *Cupid* worked as a trawler, but was eventually sold for £55 in 1896 and broken up by Seago and Company at Yarmouth.

THE PADDLE TUG *EXPRESS*, C.1902

The largest tug company in Yarmouth was the Great Yarmouth Steam Tug Company Ltd., formed in 1880, and owner of the Red Funnel Tugs. The photograph shows *Express*, built at South Shields in 1872, towing out four smacks at the harbour bend in the early days of the century. Other tugs in this company included *United Service, Meteor, Victoria, Star* and *Yare*. Express was broken up in 1906

THE PADDLE TUG *TOM PERRY*, c.1900

Paddle tugs were a common sight in Yarmouth harbour at the turn of the century. The photograph shows good views of *Tom Perry* towing out a topsail schooner at the harbour entrance. *Tom Perry* was built in 1879 at South Shields and owned by Nicholson's Towage Ltd., of Yarmouth. All their tugs had white funnels with black tops. Sold back to South Shields in 1907, she was finally broken up in 1920.

THE *FLYING CHILDERS* AND SMACK *BETSY*, JUNE 1896

The paddle tug *Flying Childers* lays alongside the smack *Betsy* YH 466. Both were owned by E.A. Durrant of South Quay, Yarmouth. The *Betsy* was bringing in trawl fish for shipment to Billingsgate Market when she was in collision with the pleasure steamer *Yarmouth* on June 5th 1896. The smack is obviously badly damaged on her bow and has been towed to Durrant's Quay by the *Flying Childers*.

THE PADDLE TUG *YARE* WITH PASSENGERS, c.1896

Seaward bound with passengers, the paddle tug *Yare* passes South Quay about 1896. Sea trips to Lowestoft, Cromer and Southwold were very popular in season. Built in 1883 at Beeching Brothers, the *Yare* was one of only three paddle tugs built at Yarmouth, surviving until July 1927 when lost on Scroby Sands. The sailing trawler YH 987 is *Renown* built 1876 and one of the E.A. Durrant fleet of over thirty trawling vessels.

SS. EDWARD VII IN YARMOUTH HARBOUR

THE PADDLE TUG *KING EDWARD VII*, c.1910

The paddle tug *King Edward VII* leaving harbour with passengers about 1910. The *King Edward VII* was one of the last paddle tugs built and she arrived at Yarmouth on June 28th, 1901. Built of steel and owned by Nicholson's Towage Ltd., of South Quay, *King Edward VII* was eventually sold to Sunderland owners in 1919. She was finally scrapped in 1952.

GEORGE JEWSON **ASSISTING STEAM DRIFTER, 1910**

The first tug owned by the Great Yarmouth Port and Haven Commissioners was the *George Jewson,* built at Falmouth, Cornwall in 1908. She is seen here with open wheelhouse assisting the Banff steam drifter *Pisces* BF 882 at Yarmouth in October 1910. Later *George Jewson* had an enclosed wheelhouse. Retired by the Commissioners in 1952, she was eventually broken up by a Leeds firm in 1957.

THAMES SAILING BARGES BEING TOWED OUT, 1927

Thames sailing barges were a regular source of income for the Yarmouth tug companies. The steam tug is *Tactful* which replaced the sunken paddle tug *Yare* in September 1927. She is seen here in October 1934 towing out *Ethel Everard* and another barge. *Ethel Everard* was built at Fellows Yard, Southtown, in 1926. The *Tactful* performed useful service for her owners until sold to owners on the south coast in April 1938.

DIESEL TUG *HECTOR READ*, 1974

The diesel tug *Hector Read* near the harbour entrance in November 1974. She replaced the steam tug *Richard Lee Barber* in 1965. Built at Grimsby and used by the Great Yarmouth Port and Haven Commissioners, now called the Great Yarmouth Port Authority, she is now the sole tug in the port of Great Yarmouth. In the 1880s when the fishing fleet of smacks was at its peak, some sixteen local paddle tugs were operating out of Yarmouth with additions from other ports in the herring season.

ALL SET FOR THE NORFOLK BROADS, c.1906

Three Broads excursion steamers preparing to leave Stonecutters Quay, Yarmouth for river trips about 1906. Nearest is *Lily,* loading passengers for Burgh Castle and the Roman ruins, ahead of her is *Pride of the Yare,* sister vessel to the *Queen of the Broads,* and furthest away is *Waterfly,* owned by the Long family. Both the latter vessels regularly ran in season to St. Olaves and Norwich. Remains of the *Waterfly* can still be seen along the Breydon Water South Wall just under one mile from Yarmouth.

THE *SOUTHTOWN* AT SOUTH QUAY, 1899

The steamer *Southtown,* built 1896 at Fellows Yard, Southtown, under the supervision of Thomas Bradley, manager of the Yarmouth and Gorleston Steamboat Company. Licensed originally for 322 passengers, she is seen here in 1899 about to leave South Quay for Gorleston. The return trip to Gorleston in those days was four old pence. A single trip was twopence and an extra penny was charged to sit on the upper deck. Initially the Yarmouth to Gorleston steamers except for the *Lily* and *Resolute* ran in connection with the tram cars.

Gorleston Quay

THE *SOUTHTOWN* AT GORLESTON, c.1910

Another view of *Southtown* laying at the Gorleston end of the journey, the landing stage at Pier Walk. This vessel operated on the Gorleston to Yarmouth run all her life apart from a brief spell from 1918 when moved to Southampton for three years to help on the Hythe to Southampton ferry crossings. Southtown, along with *Cobholm, Gorleston, Yarmouth, Resolute* and *Oulton Belle* had screw propulsion at each end of the vessel. *Southtown* was finally broken up in 1965 in Holland.

Copyright.

The Steamer landing Passengers—Burgh Castle.

LANDING PASSENGERS AT BURGH CASTLE, c.1905

The *Lily* with passengers at Burgh Castle about 1905. The *Lily* was the original Yarmouth to Gorleston passenger steamer and built at Bristol in 1894. Owned by the Pioneer Steamship Company, *Lily* began trips to Burgh Castle in 1903 costing nine old pence and children under 12 were charged six old pence. These summer excursions continued until 1912 when *Lily* was converted into a barge.

THE RIVER-BOATS, GORLESTON.

THE YARMOUTH TO GORLESTON RIVER SERVICE, c.1912

The steamers *Southtown* (on left) and *Cobholm* (on right) with passengers along the River Yare between Yarmouth and Gorleston about 1912. *Cobholm* was built in 1900 at Fellows Yard, Southtown for the Yarmouth and Gorleston Steamboat Company Limited. She had an upper deck for her crew, but unlike *Southtown* or *Resolute* carried no passengers on this deck. These sailing between Yarmouth and Gorleston finished in 1961 and *Cobholm* was sold to Holland to be broken up.

3772 The Landing Stage, Gorleston.

THE LANDING STAGE AT GORLESTON, 1920s

The landing stage at Gorleston with the steamer *Resolute* landing passengers from Yarmouth in the 1920s. Originally owned by the Pioneer Steamship Company, the *Resolute* was purchased in 1919 by the Yarmouth and Gorleston Steamboat Company Limited. When built in 1903, she cost £2,600 and was licensed for 312 passengers. The landing stage at the bottom of Pier Walk, Gorleston, was a feature for many years, but has now been filled in. On the Yarmouth side, the herring export sheds are clearly visible.

DAY TRIPPERS READY FOR EXCURSION, JUNE 1938

Day trippers line up on deck of the pleasure steamer, *Pride of the Yare* at Stonecutters Quay in June 1938. Pleasure trips on the Norfolk Broads were especially popular from Yarmouth for many years, with regular cruises to Wroxham, Norwich, Oulton Broad and Beccles. The best known and favourite vessel was *Queen of the Broads,* built at Cobholm Island in 1889 for Thomas Bradley. She was lengthened in 1896 to accommodate extra passengers. *Queen of the Broads* was broken up in 1976 at Lake Lothing, Oulton Broad, after carrying many thousands of holiday-makers on Norfolk Broad cruises.

CREW OF THE *OULTON BELLE* 1930s

Crew of the *Oulton Belle* at Yarmouth in the 1930s. *Oulton Belle* was a steam vessel built at Fellows Yard, Southtown, in 1930 for the Yarmouth and Gorleston Steamboat Company Limited. Used mainly for river and broads trips, *Oulton Belle* was also used on the Yarmouth to Gorleston run. Sold in 1954 to Scarborough she was renamed the *Regal Lady* and operated sea trips. In October 1970, she returned to run trips from Norwich along the River Yare until 1984. *Regal Lady* returned to Scarborough in January 1987.

S.S. RESOLUTE OF GT. YARMOUTH.

THE *RESOLUTE* ON BREYDON WATER, 1950s

The *Resolute* passing through the old Breydon Viaduct in the 1950s. The *Resolute* arrived at Yarmouth from London in 1903 to replace the *Lily* on the Yarmouth to Gorleston river run. In 1946 *Resolute* began broads trips mainly along the River Waveney to St. Olaves and often in competition with the larger *Golden Galleon*. Sold in 1967 to the Veteran Steamship Society, she is presently on the River Orwell at Shotley awaiting possible restoration.

Golden Galleon LEAVING HAVEN BRIDGE QUAY FOR BROADS CRUISE

GOLDEN GALLEON AND BREYDON VIADUCT, c.1956

The *Golden Galleon* passing through the old Breydon Water viaduct about 1956. This viaduct built at the turn of the century was demolished in April 1962. *Golden Galleon* was built in 1940 as an Admiralty Fairmile B Motor Launch ML 162. In 1950 she ran sea trips and broads trips. *Golden Galleon* is still in operation today running Broads trips from Stonecutters Quay.

A CROWDED SOUTH QUAY WITH LONDON STEAMERS, c.1910

A typical scene at Yarmouth South Quay prior to the First World War, probably taken at the weekend, shows *Southend Belle* preparing to sail, with *Walton Belle* in the background awaiting her passengers. The Belle boats regularly called at Lowestoft, Southwold, Clacton and Southend on route for London and were very popular for many years. The first Belle boat to arrive was *Walton Belle* in June 1897.

LONDON BOATS AT SOUTH QUAY, c.1904

Two of the General Steam Navigation Company's London vessels at South Quay about 1904. Loaded with passengers and preparing to sail is *Mavis* while just inside of her is another of the "Classical Birds" probably the *Laverock*. These vessels, unlike the Belle steamers, ran a direct service to London and were generally slower than their counterparts. *Laverock* was scrapped in 1912 and *Mavis* three years later.

THE *YARMOUTH BELLE* ARRIVES, c.1905

The *Yarmouth Belle* arrives with passengers from London. Built in 1898 at Dumbarton and owned by the Coast Development Company, *Yarmouth Belle* was a regular visitor in season. She was almost identical with the *Walton Belle* built the previous year. A smaller pleasure steamer of the same name built at Yarmouth in 1892 ran trips on the Norfolk Broads from Yarmouth during the same period. She was, however, not a paddle vessel.

V332-18   THE YARMOUTH BELLE.   RAPID PHOTO. E.C.

THE *YARMOUTH BELLE* AT SOUTH QUAY, c.1905

Another view of *Yarmouth Belle* loaded with passengers as she prepares to moor at South Quay in the early days of the present century. A smart vessel indeed, *Yarmouth Belle* had a chequered career and served as a minesweeper in the First World War. Later renamed *Queen of Southend* in 1929 and owned by the new Medway Steam Packet Company (The "Queen Line"), this grand old lady was finally scrapped at Dover in 1948.

BELLE STEAMER AT GORLESTON-ON-SEA.

BELLE STEAMER AT GORLESTON, c.1910

The Belle steamers plying to London and back, stopped at Gorleston to pick up passengers from 1905 onwards. The postcard shows one of the vessels laying by the King William the Fourth Public House at the bottom of Pier Walk. The local agent for these Belle steamers was Harry Lee who at the time had a tobacconist's shop opposite The Feathers Inn at Gorleston.

LORD NELSON LEAVING SOUTH QUAY, c.1905

Sea trips were a "must" for visitors staying at Yarmouth. The *Lord Nelson* pleasure steamer is seen leaving her town hall moorings about 1905 for Lowestoft. The *Lord Nelson,* built in 1896 at Preston, was owned by the Great Yarmouth Steam Tug Company Ltd. After useful service, she was sold to French owners in January 1913. These Lowestoft trips in 1904 were twice daily in season and cost 1s 3d (6 new pence) one way, and 1s 9d (9 new pence) return.

LORD NELSON ENTERING HARBOUR, c.1904

Another view of the paddle pleasure steamer *Lord Nelson* entering harbour from Lowestoft about 1904. *Lord Nelson* and her sister vessel the *Lord Roberts* were known locally as the butterfly boats as they both were used only for the summer season. In winter, both laid upstream of the Haven Bridge. Between 1896 and 1899, *Lord Nelson* also ran summer trips to Southwold, landing her passengers on the beach.

SEA TRIPS IN THE 1930s

Sea trips aboard the paddle steam tug *United Service* were popular in the 1930s. Her passengers pose for the cameraman of "Jackson Faces" prior to her sea trip around the bell buoy, Scroby Sands and *St. Nicholas* lightship. These in-season sea trips began in the 1860s and ceased in 1939 when *United Service* was sold to the breaker's yard. She was eventually broken up in 1942.

WHERRIES AT SOUTHTOWN, c.1880

Wherries laying three abreast in Yarmouth harbour about 1880. Also laying on the Southtown side of the river in this view is the small Scandinavian schooner *Marie Sophie* and a spritsail barge. The local trawling smacks are much in evidence on the east side of the river. Despite the fish wharf's opening in 1867, many trawlers continued to land their catches for several years at the south end of South Quay, much to the annoyance of residents there.

AN IRON WHERRY BEING LAUNCHED AT SOUTHTOWN, 1898

A rare view of a wherry being launched. This is *Sirius,* an iron wherry sliding down the slipway in 1898 from the Southtown Yard of Fellows & Company for Woods, Sadd, Moore & Company of Loddon. The trawler smack alongside the Quay is *Queen Bess* YH 1050, built by Henry Critten, Cobholm Island, for the trawling fleet of F.S. and J. Leleu of London. Her last Yarmouth owner was W.J. Laws of Row 124.

WHERRIES IN THE RIVER BURE PRIOR TO 1896

Trading wherries laying in the River Bure above the suspension bridge at Yarmouth prior to 1896. The north-west Tower and White Swan Public House can be seen in the background. Exactly opposite this site, the largest wherry ever built, the 80-ton *Wonder,* was launched in 1878 for William Smith of the Suspension Bridge Public House. She was designed with the special objective of being sent out to sea to load from ships too large to get into harbour.

SAILING BARGES AND THE SOUTHTOWN MALTINGS, c.1904

Thames sailing barges and other sailing vessels moored alongside the Southtown Maltings of Watney, Combe and Reid just after the turn of the century. The barge on the left is *Alice May* of Ipswich, built at Harwich in 1898. Note the passengers waiting at the lower ferry, a rowing boat taking them in those days to the Southtown side. Up to the outbreak of the First World War, four ferries were at work along the River Yare at Yarmouth.

THE THAMES BARGE *CAMBRIA*, 1971

The last Thames sailing barge, *Cambria,* built at Greenhithe, Kent, in 1906 being towed through the Haven Bridge on July 2nd 1971 after a trip to Norwich. The *Cambria* was well known at Yarmouth for many years, being owned by the firm of Everards until purchased in 1966 by her long-time skipper Bob Roberts. In 1971, she was purchased by the Maritime Trust of London and is at present preserved at Sittingbourne in Kent.

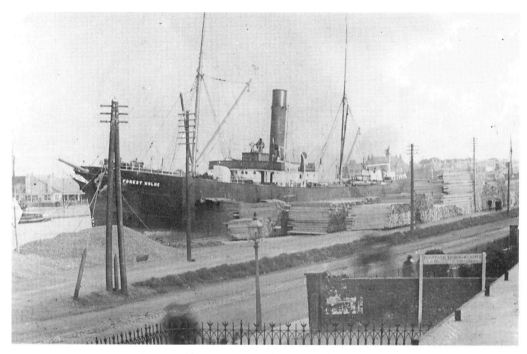

BOLLARD QUAY, SOUTHTOWN, c.1895

The British steamer *Forest Holme* unloading her cargo of timber from Scandinavia at Bollard Quay, Southtown, just before the turn of the century. Southtown Road appears to be unmade and the sign in the bottom right-hand corner of the photograph reads, "Footpath to Burgh Castle, 5 miles to the Ruins". The sign is situated at the eastern end of Boundary Road where it joins Southtown Road. At the western end of Boundary Road the Spotted Cow Public House once stood, but this was destroyed by a bomb in the Second World War.

The %"Pearlmoor"
from Mobile
at Messrs Jewsons' Quay G. Yarmouth.

THE TIMBER VESSEL *PEARLMOOR* AT JEWSON'S QUAY, 1912

The London-registered steamer *Pearlmoor* with timber from Mobile, Alabama, at Jewson's Quay, Southtown, in 1912. The *Pearlmoor* was a turret ship, a vessel without any sheer, that is to say there is no vertical curve in the ship's deckline between bow and stern. Bottom left is the upper ferry boat rowing across from South Quay to Southtown. This ferry closed in 1954, but the steps on the Southtown side remained for some years, finally being demolished in 1972.

BOLLARD QUAY, SOUTHTOWN, c.1950

Bollard Quay, Southtown about 1950. A Norwegian motor timber vessel unloads her cargo onto the quayside by Southtown Road. The Bollard Quay was used for many years for the storage of timber for the main Yarmouth timber-importing firms of Jewson and Sons Ltd., and Palgrave Brown Ltd., whose premises can be seen in the background. Jewson no longer import timber into Yarmouth and the Palgrave Brown premises closed in October 1985.

THE *MADONNA* OF YARMOUTH, APRIL 1953

A view from South Quay April 1953. A timber vessel is unloading at Jewson and Sons Ltd. Quay on the west side of the river with a steel lighter alongside to take part of the cargo up river, presumably to Norwich. The *Madonna* of Yarmouth moored at South Quay was an ex-corvette owned by Henry Sutton Ltd., for refrigerated trips to the Mediterranean with herrings. She was sold in January 1954 to New Zealand after a complete refit in Fellows Dock, Southtown.

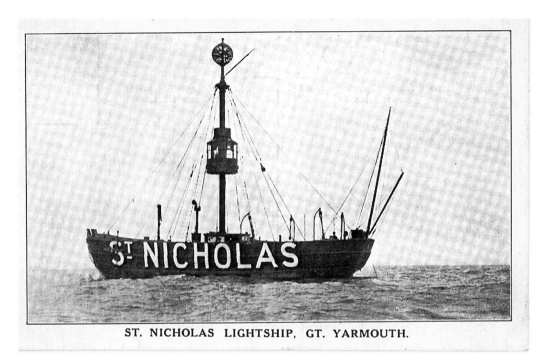

ST. NICHOLAS LIGHTSHIP, GT. YARMOUTH.

THE *ST. NICHOLAS* LIGHTSHIP (OR VESSEL), c.1910

An older-style light vessel, the *St. Nicholas* was stationed a short distance off the Yarmouth harbour entrance until the outbreak of the Second World War. Pleasure sea trips regularly ran from Yarmouth harbour around her and the *Cockle* light vessel stationed further north towards Caister. Many of these old vessels were brought in during the last war and moored upstream of the Haven Bridge. Most were later broken up.

TENDER TOWING LIGHT VESSEL, c.1900

A Trinity House tender, almost certainly the *Argus,* built 1856, towing out the *Leman and Ower* light vessel from Yarmouth about 1900. The *Argus* started life as a paddle steamer, but was later converted to twin screw propulsion. The *Argus* was broken up in 1909 after a long and useful service for Trinity House. The *Leman and Ower* light vessel was stationed a considerable distance to the north-east of Great Yarmouth.

ROWING TO THE CORTON LIGHT VESSEL, c.1900

A Trinity House boarding party from the Trinity steamer row out to the *Corton* light vessel which was stationed about six miles south-east of Gorleston. The photograph, about 1900, shows it to be one of the older wooden standard light vessels. For many years, Beeching Brothers Shipyard at Yarmouth had the contract to overhaul these vessels, a handy arrangement as the Yarmouth Trinity House Depot was next door.

THE CROSS SAND LIGHT VESSEL, 1974

The *Cross Sand* light vessel No.22 at Trinity Wharf Yarmouth on May 16th, 1974. A very modern type of light vessel, No.22 was built at Richard's Shipyard at Lowestoft in 1967, one of the last light vessels built. Although shipyards at Yarmouth built a variety of vessels, no light vessel was ever built along the banks of the Yare. The *Cross Sand's* position was some twelve miles due east of Yarmouth and the light vessel itself was replaced by a fixed buoy and light in 1975.

THE DREDGER *FITZROY* AT SOUTHTOWN, c.1890

The steam dredger *Fitzroy* moored on the Southtown side of the river close to the lower ferry about 1890. Built in London, she arrived in Yarmouth in April 1879 in tow of the steam tug *Punch*. She was named after the chairman of the Port and Haven Commissioners Hugh Fitzroy. The *Fitzroy* had a crew of seven and on trial raised 360 tons of mud in $3^1/_2$ hours. She cost £5,647 when new and was sold in 1904.

THE DREDGER *SIR HARRY BULLARD*, 1905

The *Sir Harry Bullard,* a twin screw steam dredger replaced the *Fitzroy* in June 1904. She was built at Glasgow at a cost of about £15,000 and is seen here dredging close to the Haven Bridge. Named after the late chairman of the Port and Haven Commissioners, she proved too big and powerful for the River Yare. In 1906 she was sold and crossed the Atlantic where she was employed in the workings for the Isthmian Canal, Panama.

DREDGER ON DARBY'S HARD AT GORLESTON, 1930s

The small Yarmouth dredger barge laying on Darby's Hard, Gorleston in the 1930s. This barge was converted into a dredger, her stern being cut off on the Spending beach in 1902, and a steam crane and machinery fitted by the firm of Preistman of Hull at Gorleston Quayside. She was employed mainly for dredging close to the quays with a fleet of hopper barges alongside. This barge was still at work in the early 1960s.

SUBMARINES STUCK ACROSS THE HAVEN BRIDGE, 1908

Navy submarines Nos. 32 and 35 stuck across the old Haven Bridge on May 17th, 1908. These two submarines were part of a flotilla of four attempting to moor at the Hall Quay when a strong flood tide swept them against the bridge. The previous year, the same flotilla of submarines plus the attendant cruiser *Thames* put into Yarmouth in late August, moored near the Southtown ferry and visited by many people.

CAISTER LIFEBOATS ON BEACH, c.1895

Caister beach just before the turn of the century with beach yawls and lifeboats. The nearest lifeboat on the right behind a yawl is *Beauchamp,* the Caister No.2 lifeboat, built at Critten's Yard, Yarmouth, in 1892. In November 1901, *Beauchamp* overturned in the breakers with the loss of nine of her crew. She was broken up in 1966, having spent her last years at the rear of Gorleston library.

Gt. Yarmouth Lifeboat Crew.   Copyright.

LIFEBOAT *JOHN BURCH* AND CREW, c.1905

Yarmouth lifeboat *John Burch* and crew pose for the cameraman along Yarmouth seafront about 1905. *John Burch,* a rowing and sailing type lifeboat with 12 oars was built by Beeching Brothers of Yarmouth in 1892. She was on station at Yarmouth from 1892 to May 1912. This lifeboat was then sold to a Mr. Johnson in June 1912 for £18. She was later converted and become a houseboat on the river Waveney at St. Olaves.

LAUNCHING GT. YARMOUTH LIFEBOAT.

LAUNCHING GREAT YARMOUTH LIFEBOAT, c.1905

Another view of the Yarmouth lifeboat *John Burch,* a surf lifeboat of the Norfolk and Suffolk type being launched from central beach in the early days of the century. *John Burch* was presented to the RNLI in May 1892 and built at the expense of Mrs. Burch, Sir H. Tyler MP and Sir Edward Birkbeck MP. She replaced the lifeboat *Abraham Thomas* which had been in use at Yarmouth for some 33 years.

GREAT YARMOUTH LIFEBOAT *HUGH TAYLOR* AND CREW, c.1913

The last Yarmouth lifeboat, *Hugh Taylor,* and crew on central beach, probably about 1913. Built at Blackwall on the River Thames, *Hugh Taylor* arrived at Yarmouth on May 14th 1912 in tow of a steam trawler. The Yarmouth lifeboat station closed in 1919 and *Hugh Taylor* later saw RNLI service at Pakefield, Kessingland and Aldeburgh. The old lifeboat shed remained open to the public for exhibition purposes and housed the small lifeboat *James Finlayson* until it also closed in October 1932.

"THE CALL TO DUTY", c.1900

The Gorleston Ranger Company volunteer lifeboat *Elizabeth Simpson* being launched at low water from her riverside shed about the turn of the century. Waiting in the background to tow her out to sea is the paddle tug *United Service*. The Yarmouth harbour tugs often helped the local lifeboats out to casualties at sea. Built in 1889 at Beeching's Yard, Yarmouth, *Elizabeth Simpson* remained in service until 1939.

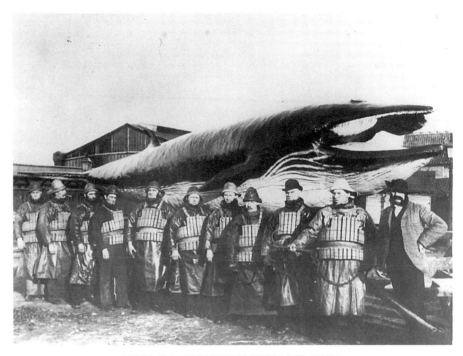

THE GORLESTON WHALE, 1891

Gorleston Ranger lifeboatmen with the seven-ton lesser rorqual whale captured in the harbour on June 8th, 1891. The whale was 30 feet in length and 18½ feet in circumference. It was hauled up in the Ranger lifeboat shed tail first and, after considerable work from local taxidermist Walter Lowne, was exhibited by naturalist Arthur Patterson (John Knowlittle) in London, Norwich, Lowestoft and finally Yarmouth the following year.

"ELIZABETH SIMPSON" LIFEBOAT, GORLESTON-ON-SEA.

THE *ELIZABETH SIMPSON* ENTERING HARBOUR, c.1928

The *Elizabeth Simpson* volunteer lifeboat was fitted with an engine during 1926 and ran passenger sea trips from Brush Quay, Gorleston during the summer months. She is seen here entering harbour with a full compliment of passengers with the North Pier in the background. Such excursions earned a little extra revenue for hard-pressed funds.

THE *ELIZABETH SIMPSON* AS A PLEASURE CRAFT, 1982

The now converted ex-lifeboat *Elizabeth Simpson* alongside the Haven Bridge in August 1982. Owned by Pleasure Steamers Ltd., she ran trips along the River Waveney and to Burgh Castle and Berney Arms. The raised wheelhouse was added in 1980. *Elizabeth Simpson* is presently based at Potter Heigham, but her future is very uncertain. It would be a fitting tribute to see her preserved, and especially in her old shed at Gorleston, which still stands.

THE *VAUBAN* ASHORE ON YARMOUTH BEACH, 1888

Several onlookers discussed the prospects of the sailing barque *Vauban* from Le Havre ashore on Yarmouth beach just south of the Wellington Pier on November 4th 1888. The *Vauban* came ashore with a broken back and several days later the sails and rigging had been removed. She was eventually broken up. Her crew of fifteen had earlier been rescued by the Caister lifeboat *Covent Garden*.

A SAILING BARQUE ASHORE, 1905

The sailing barque *Erna* ashore at the North Pier at the entrance to Yarmouth harbour on November 11th, 1905. The *Erna's* eight-man crew were rescued by the Yarmouth Lifeboat *John Burch*. As the *Erna* fell apart, an amazing sight was witnessed: literally hundreds of rats swam ashore and for a short time changed the colour of part of South Beach to black. The *Erna* was a regular visitor to Yarmouth.

A NORWEGIAN BARQUE ASHORE, 1910

Well ashore on Yarmouth North Beach, the Norwegian barque *Ceres* on October 22nd, 1910. Previously adrift by the Scroby Sands, *Ceres* ran aground during the night. With her holds full of water, she wallowed in the breakers for some time as each wave hit her, and eventually broke her back. A few days later a gale smashed *Ceres* to pieces, her cargo of timber littering the beaches for miles.

THE *CORONILLA* AT GORLESTON, 1907

The steam ship *Coronilla* of North Shields laying at Darby's Hard, Gorleston, February 1907. A large hole in her starboard side close to the bows is most obvious. *Coronilla* was in collision with the Liverpool liner *Virginian* in thick fog in the vicinity of *Newarp* light vessel on February 22nd and was towed into Yarmouth by two tugs the next day. She was originally on passage from the Tyne to Dunkirk. Shipwrights from Fellows and Company, Southtown, patched her up and *Coronilla* was towed away to drydock on the Tyne.

LOWESTOFT TRAWLER ASHORE, 1911

A little boy looks on as the Lowestoft trawling smack *Wave Crest* LT 744 is ashore near Wellington Pier on July 22nd 1911. *Wave Crest* was built at Rye the previous year and belonged to Mr. Boardley of Lowestoft. The skipper did not engage two Yarmouth tugs in attendance but waited until the Lowestoft tug *Lowestoft* arrived. On the top of the flood tide, the *Wave Crest* was successfully towed off.

STEAM DRIFTER SUNK IN HARBOUR, 1911

The Banff steam drifter *Forward* BF 624 sunk in the river close to the harbour entrance on November 2nd, 1911. *Forward* was built at Lowestoft and although registered at Banff, was owned at Buckie. She was in collision with a larger Hull drifter/trawler, the *Majestic. Forward* was finally raised after considerable difficulty several days later and taken to Beeching's dry dock for survey. In the background, a steam drifter arrives from sea with caution.